Inside the NFL

THE
CHICAGO
BEARS

BOB ITALIA
ABDO & Daughters

Published by Abdo & Daughters, 4940 Viking Drive, Suite 622, Edina, Minnesota 55435.

Copyright © 1996 by Abdo Consulting Group, Inc., Pentagon Tower, P.O. Box 36036, Minneapolis, Minnesota 55435 USA. International copyrights reserved in all countries. No part of this book may be reproduced in any form without written permission from the publisher.

Printed in the United States.

Edited by Kal Gronvall

Library of Congress Cataloging-in-Publication Data

Italia, Bob, 1955
        The Chicago Bears / Bob Italia.
        p.   cm. — (Inside the NFL)
Includes index.
Summary: Describes the origin, history, and traditions of the football team known as the "Monsters of the Midway."
ISBN 1-56239-458-4
1. Chicago Bears (Football team)—History—Juvenile literature. [1. Chicago Bears (Football team)—History. 2. Football—History.] I. Title. II. Series: Italia, Bob, 1955- Inside the NFL.
GV956.C5I83   1995
796.332'64'09—dc20   95-2444
                                                              CIP
                                                              AC

CONTENTS

The Birth of the NFL

More than any other professional football team, the Chicago Bears are responsible for making the National Football League (NFL) the national treasure that it is today.

Professional football's fortunes changed when Bears' owner George Halas signed legendary running back Red Grange to a contract in 1925. Then he sent his team on a nationwide tour. As a result, pro football captured sports fans of all ages. From that time, professional football has only gained in popularity.

George Halas, legendary owner/coach of the Chicago Bears, exhorts his players during the final minutes against the New York Giants.

The Bears have a rich tradition of winning championships with a ferocious defense and a strong running game. Some of the NFL's greatest players have worn a Bears jersey. Players like Bronco Nagurski, Dick Butkus, Gale Sayers, Doug Atkins, Walter Payton, Dan Hampton, Richard Dent, and Mike Singletary have, throughout the decades, entertained and amazed football fans with their power, speed, and athletic ability.

The Bears have also fashioned some of the greatest teams in NFL history. And they have played in some of its most memorable games—including the 1940 and 1985 routs in the championship games. Though the current Bears have not yet reached championship form, it is only a matter of time until the "Monsters of the Midway" roar again.

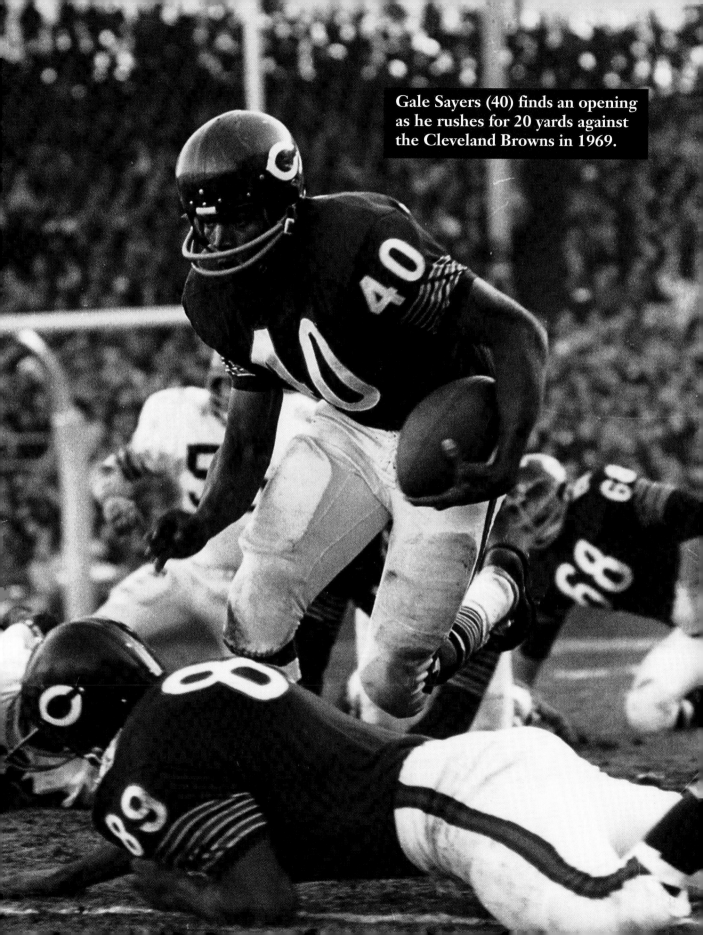

Gale Sayers (40) finds an opening as he rushes for 20 yards against the Cleveland Browns in 1969.

The Decatur Staleys

The Bears began their long history in a quiet way. Born in Chicago, Illinois in 1895, George Halas formed the Decatur Staleys professional football team in 1920. In 1921, the Staley Starch Company of Decatur, Illinois, ended its sponsorship of the team. George Halas and his partner, Dutch Sternaman, bought the team outright. They moved it to Chicago and renamed the club the Chicago Bears. Five years later, Halas gained complete control of the club.

Halas did everything to make the Bears successful. He sold tickets, managed equipment, took care of the playing field, and coached. In one game, he played defensive end. When running back Jim Thorpe fumbled the ball, Halas scooped it up and raced a record 98 yards for a Chicago touchdown.

"Papa Bear" Halas was the first NFL coach to hold daily practices and study game films. Halas also changed the name of the American Professional Football Association to the NFL. He knew that one day the game would become a national treasure. To help him achieve his goal, Halas signed two well-known running backs who changed the future of the Chicago Bears and the NFL.

The Galloping Ghost

The first of these two running backs was Red Grange, an All-American halfback from the University of Illinois. Grange earned his nickname, the "Galloping Ghost," by scoring five touchdowns the first five times he carried the ball for his team against the University of Michigan in 1924. He also scored an amazing 31 touchdowns in his three-year college football career. In those three short years, Grange had become a superstar. Now he was ready for professional football.

Halas was right there with a shiny pen and dollar signs in his eyes. He signed Grange on November 22, 1925, and immediately started a football tour from New York to Los Angeles to show off his new star. The Bears played football in 19 cities in less than six months. They attracted over 350,000 football fans. Grange has now established professional football as a nationwide success.

Red Grange earned his nickname, the "Galloping Ghost," by scoring five touchdowns against Michigan in 1924.

Grange played professional football in Chicago for 13 seasons. But because accurate records were not kept in the 1920s, Grange is not listed among the Bears' top 25 all-time rushers. Still, Grange had more impact on professional football than any other player in its long history.

Bronco

The second famous running back, Bronislau "Bronco" Nagurski, joined the Bears for the 1930 season. "Bronco" became an all-star that same year. Nagurski played seven seasons for Chicago. His powerful running style made him a fan favorite.

Between 1932 and 1934 Chicago dominated the NFL. They won two consecutive championships (1932 and 1933). The Bears were the class of the NFL.

But toward the end of the 1930s, the Bears faded. Future Hall-of-Famers Nagurski and Grange were battered veterans. Their careers were coming to an end.

Halas needed a new star to lead the Bears to the top. He signed Sid Luckman and made him into a quarterback.

Luckman had played his college ball as a tailback at Columbia University. He knew the T formation well and ran it to perfection. From 1940 to 1943, Luckman led the Bears to an amazing 37-5-1 record.

"Bronco" Nagurski played seven seasons for Chicago. His powerful running style made him a fan favorite.

73-0

In 1963, the National Academy of Sports Editors voted the 1940 Chicago Bears as the greatest professional team of all time. It was the 1940 championship game that won them many votes.

That year, the Bears had played the Washington Redskins and lost 7-3 on a questionable call. When the Bears protested, the Redskins' owner, George Marshall, told the press that "the Bears were quitters and a bunch of cry babies."

Coach Halas was furious. He tacked up the newspaper article throughout the locker room. Halas then gave an inspirational talk.

"Gentlemen," Halas said, "this is what the Redskins think of you. I think you're a great football team, the greatest ever assembled. Go out onto the field and prove it."

The Bears destroyed the Redskins 73-0 before 36,000 disbelieving Redskins fans. At one point late in the game, an official asked Halas not to kick any more extra points. Too many extra-point footballs had been kicked into the stands. The Redskins were down to their last football!

The 1940 championship game wasn't just a fluke. Those Bears had three future Hall of Famers on their team—Luckman, George McAfee, and Joe Stydahar. The record 73 points still stands today as the most points scored in any NFL regular-season, playoff, or championship game. Some observers said the 1940 Bears were a perfect football team. But Halas disagreed. He thought they should have scored more points against the Giants.

From 1947 to 1951, the Bears had more winning seasons. But injuries stopped them from winning more championship games. Luckman retired in 1951. Fourteen years later, he was named to the Hall of Fame.

Rebuilding the Bears

From 1952 to 1962, the Bears were no longer one of the NFL's top teams. Star players like Rick Casares, Willie Galimore, and Bobby Watkins could not win another championship. Halas had quit coaching so he could manage the business side of the team. But Halas was tired of losing. It was time to coach again.

Almost immediately, the Bears started winning again. In 1963, defensive coach George Allen designed a zone pass defense that made the Bears' defense the toughest in the NFL. In each game, the Bears' defense allowed only 10 points. This ferocious defense grew famous by winning games without much offensive help.

Doug Atkins, Ed O'Bradovich, Bill George, Joe Fortunato, Larry Morris, Richie Petitbon, and Rosey Taylor were the stars. Johnny Morris, Billy Wade, and Mike Ditka led the offense. They often ran safe running plays and threw short passes to eliminate turnovers and mistakes.

By the end of the 1963 season, the Bears had finished one-half game ahead of the Green Bay Packers. In the title game against the New York Giants, the Bears were underdogs. Quarterback Y. A. Tittle and running back Frank Gifford starred for the favored Giants. Both were considered among the best players in the NFL. Few experts gave the Bears a chance to win the game.

But the Bears' ferocious defense forced the Giants into many mistakes. Intercepting five of Tittle's passes, the Bears defeated the Giants 14-10. It was the Bears' first championship in 17 years.

In 1964, injuries hurt the Bears defense. The preseason deaths of Willie Galimore and Bo Farrington weakened the offense. The Bears lost three of their first four games. Eventually, they fell to the bottom of the Western conference.

Sayers and Butkus

In 1965, the Bears turned their misfortunes around. That season's draft was one of the best ever for the Bears—or for any NFL team. Halas signed linebacker Dick Butkus from the University of Illinois. He also landed running back Gale Sayers from the University of Kansas.

Both Sayers and Butkus turned in All-Pro rookie seasons. Sayers excelled as kick returner, pass receiver, and running back. He scored a record 22 touchdowns for the season.

Sayers was elected to the Hall in his first year of eligibility. Though a knee injury cut short his seven-year career, each season Sayers put on an offensive show with his blinding speed and shifty moves. In all, he gained nearly 5,000 yards rushing.

Meanwhile, Butkus struck fear in the hearts of opponents with his ferocious tackling and hard-nosed play. In 1979, Butkus was also inducted into the Hall of Fame in his first year of eligibility. During his career, Butkus was All-Pro eight times and played in eight Pro Bowls.

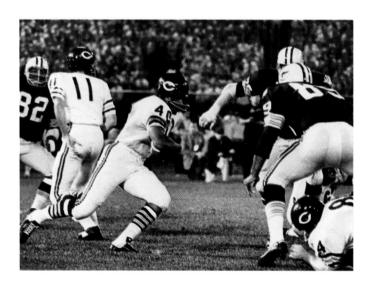

Gale Sayers excelled as kick returner, pass receiver, and running back. He scored a record 22 touchdowns his rookie season.

Dick Butkus struck fear in the hearts of opponents with his ferocious tackling and hard-nosed play.

Slumbering Bears

From the late 1960s through most of the 1970s, the Bears went into hibernation. Players like Butkus, Sayers, and quarterback Vince Evans remained the star attractions. But the supporting cast was weak and the team records slipped. Coach Abe Gibron was 11-30-1 from 1972 to 1974. Jack Pardee was 20-22 from 1975 to 1978. Fortunately for Bear fans, Chicago drafted one of the greatest backs of all time—the man they called "Sweetness." His name was Walter Payton.

Walter Payton helped make the Bears a great team again in the 1980s.

Walter Payton is among the NFL's all-time greatest running backs.

"Sweetness"

Walter Jerry Payton was born and raised in Columbia, Mississippi. He spent his childhood competing with his older brother, Eddie. Eddie was considered the athlete in the family. While Eddie played high school football, Payton played drums in the school band. He also joined the gymnastics team.

Payton was a shy young man. He often stayed in the house with his mother and read or helped her with the chores while his brother played football. But after Eddie graduated, Walter began playing football. It didn't take long for everyone to realize that Payton was good—even better than Eddie. In Payton's first high school game, he ran for a 61-yard touchdown.

Payton went to Jackson State and had an outstanding college career. Halas drafted Payton in 1975 and showed great promise his rookie season. In 1976, he showed he was a star with a great future. He won the rushing title with 1,390 yards.

One of Payton's most memorable games came in November 1977 on a cold, damp Chicago day. Over 50,000 fans jammed Chicago's Soldier Field to watch the Bears play the Minnesota Vikings. Payton rewarded them by rushing for 275 yards. He gained more rushing yardage that day than any other man had ever gained in a single game in all of professional football history. Because of his remarkable running and scoring talents, his teammates called him "sweetness."

Over the next 11 years, Payton's powerful and determined running helped him become the NFL's greatest rusher. Despite his success, Payton remained humble throughout his record-setting career. He always gave credit to his linemen for his record-setting seasons. After one game, he even gave each of them an engraved gold watch to show his appreciation.

Payton was happy about his personal success as a runner. But as an athlete in a team sport, he had not yet claimed the greatest prize of all—a Super Bowl championship.

Payton's powerful and determined running helped him become the NFL's all-time leading rusher.

Ditka

To become a great team again, the Bears needed more than a great running back. The Bears had won championships with great defenses. And Halas knew he had to find a coach who could restore the team's ferocious image and take them to the top.

In 1982, Halas hired Mike Ditka, a former Bear tight end who was an assistant coach with the Dallas Cowboys. Some experts questioned Halas' choice. They thought "Iron Mike" Ditka was too hot-tempered to coach a team. Halas disagreed. Ditka had been on the last Bear championship team (1963). He knew how to make the Bears great again. "I was always a Bear," admitted Ditka. "Even when I was playing and coaching in Dallas, I was a Chicago Bear."

Ditka brought a disciplined, hard-nosed attitude to the Bears. Having a wealth of talent with which to work made rebuilding easier. Besides Payton on offense, great players like defensive end Dan Hampton, safety Gary Fencik, and linebacker Mike Singletary anchored the team.

Before Ditka could fully restore the team's winning tradition, tragedy struck. On October 31, 1983, George Halas, the second-winningest professional coach of all time (326 wins), died of a massive heart attack. The Bears' organization had lost its founder. It would never be the same. Now the Bears had even more incentive to play hard and to win a championship.

In 1983 and 1984, Chicago captured the Central Division title. But they fell short of their ultimate goal, the Super Bowl. Winning the division wasn't good enough. They wanted more.

Despite the disappointing playoff loss to the San Francisco 49ers in the 1984 NFC championship game, Bear fans had much to cheer about. Payton had surpassed Jim Brown as the NFL's all-time leading rusher. Even more, he became the career leader in 100-yard games and set a Chicago team pass-catching mark.

The Bears knew they were good. But they needed to turn it up a notch if they wanted to win it all. With more determination than ever, the Bears set their sights on the 1985 season. They aimed high, and hit their mark—dead center.

Chicago Bears coach Mike Ditka emphasizes a point to Sylvester Byrd (95) and Tim Stracka (97) during full day workouts in 1986.

10   20   40   5

Gale Sayers turns all-pro his rookie season (1965) after scoring a record 22 touchdowns.

George Halas buys the Decatur Staleys in 1921, moves the team to Chicago, and changes the name to the Bears.

CHIC
BEA

Bronco Nagurski joins the Bears in 1930.

Red Grange signs a contract to play with the Bears in 1925.

10   20   30   40   5

40 30 20 10

Walter Payton surpasses Jim Brown in 1984 as the NFL's all-time leading rusher.

CAGO
ARS

In 1979, Dick Butkus is inducted into the Hall of Fame in his first year of eligibility.

In 1985, coach Mike Ditka leads the Bears to victory in Super Bowl XX.

CHICAGO
BEARS

40 30 20 10

Super Bears

The 1985 season turned out to be one of the all-time greatest NFL team performances. The Bears won their first 12 games and finished with a 15-1 record. The 15 wins tied an NFL mark for most wins during the regular season.

The Bears offense had an unusual cast of characters who captured national attention. Payton piled on 1,551 yards to his all-time record rushing total. Quarterback Jim McMahon became the Bears' inspirational leader and the NFC's second-best passer. And 308-pound defensive tackle William "The Refrigerator" Perry became a national hero playing fullback on short-yardage plays. Even more amazing, he also scored three touchdowns that season—one on a pass reception!

But the defense made the Bears great. Chicago led the league in fewest points allowed, rushing defense, overall defense, and interceptions. Linebackers Mike Singletary and Otis Wilson, linemen Richard Dent and Dan Hampton, and safety Dave Duerson were Pro Bowlers. Dent led the NFC in sacks for the second consecutive year with 17. Singletary, the defensive leader, was named NFL Defensive Player of the Year.

Despite their 15-1 record, the Bears weren't ready to celebrate. They had a championship to win. In the first round of the playoffs, they shutout the Washington Redskins 21-0. In the NFC championship game against the Los Angeles Rams, the fearsome Bear defense corralled Rams running back Eric Dickerson. McMahon and the offense took over and led the Bears to a 24-0 win. The final stop was New Orleans and Super Bowl XX.

It had been quite a year for the Bears. They were heavy favorites against the AFC champion New England Patriots. But until they won the big game, doubts would remain. If they won, they would place themselves amongst the top teams in NFL history. If they lost, they would be called one of the biggest flops.

The Bears were determined not to let their incredible season end in disaster. It didn't take long for the Bears to seize control of the game. After Payton fumbled deep in Bear territory, the defense stiffened and held the Patriots to a field goal. Down 3-0, the Bears regrouped and came out roaring. The growling wouldn't stop until late in the fourth quarter.

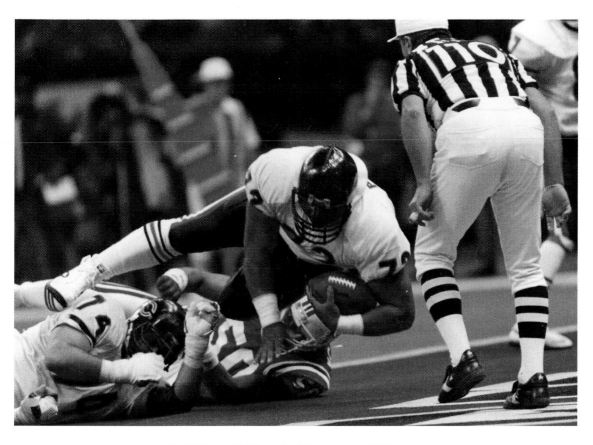

**William "The Refrigerator" Perry
finds the endzone in Super Bowl XX.**

The defense swarmed all over the Patriots while the offense played a near-perfect and imaginative game. The Bears took a 23-3 halftime lead into the locker room where they plotted for more. Meanwhile, the Bears had gained 236 total yards to the Patriots minus-14! The rout was on.

Chicago scored 21 points in the third quarter, thanks to the defense. The Patriots managed a touchdown late in the fourth quarter. But Chicago got the last laugh with a 2-point safety. The Bears won 46-10. At the time, it was the most lopsided win in Super Bowl history.

The Bears set seven Super Bowl records that night, including most points scored, and the largest margin of victory. Even William Perry found the endzone. After his thunderous spike, Perry became an overnight sensation. Though Walter Payton did not score a touchdown, he finally had his ring. No one on the Bears deserved it more.

Head coach Mike Ditka is carried off the field
after the Bears won Super Bowl XX.

Dominating the NFC Central

Between 1984 and 1988, Chicago won 62 games—the most ever by an NFL squad over a five-year span. From 1986 through 1988, the Chicago Bears dominated the NFC Central Division. They won three more division championships. Singletary, McMahon, Hampton, Payton, and Dent continued their outstanding play.

Despite their success, the Bears could not earn another Super Bowl championship. Frequent injuries to McMahon made the Bears offense inconsistent. The defense also suffered its share of injuries and lost some key players like Leslie Frazer and Otis Wilson. With the emergence of other talented teams such as the Washington Redskins and the New York Giants, the Bears defense could not dominate the league.

The Bears lost more players as the 1980s came to a close. Payton retired after the 1987 season. In 1988, All-Pro linebacker Wilbur Marshall left the team. Ditka even suffered a mild heart attack. In 1989, McMahon was traded to San Diego. The Bear dynasty was crumbling. The only bright spot that year was running back Neal Anderson. He led the team in rushing, scoring, and receiving.

The famed Bear defense shined briefly in 1990 as Hampton returned from knee surgery for his 12th and final year. Dent, Singletary, and Steve McMichael anchored the defense with outstanding play. Rookie safety Mark Carrier made the Pro Bowl with 10 interceptions that year—a team record. Chicago finished with a surprising 11-5 record and their sixth divisional title in seven years.

The Bears won 16-6 over the New Orleans Saints in the first round of the playoffs, but then were bounced 31-3 in the second round against the New York Giants.

Although the 1990 season was a success, the Bears were not the same. The defense was getting old, and the management was grumbling about Ditka's fiery sideline temper tantrums. Ditka's tactics which motivated the 1985 championship team were not working with the 1990 Bears. Something had to give.

The Bears made the playoffs in 1991 as a wild-card team, only to lose to the up-and-coming Dallas Cowboys 17-13. Chicago quarterback Jim Harbaugh set team records for most passes attempted and completed, but the team was not the same. In 1992, Chicago suffered one of the biggest collapses in their 73-year history. They lost seven of their last eight games and did not make the playoffs. Not even Mike Ditka could survive the sweeping changes made by the Bears management.

Neal Anderson led the Bears in rushing, scoring, and receiving in 1989.

The Wannstedt Era

In 1993, the Bears hired Dallas assistant coach Dave Wannstedt to replace Ditka. Wannstedt had a tough but calmer manner about him, and it worked with the new cast of young players.

Surprisingly, the Bears contended for the divisional championship until December when they lost four in a row to finish 7-9. Still, fans had reason to smile as the Bears seemed to be on the road to recovery. Middle linebacker Dante Jones and cornerback Donnell Woolford emerged as defensive stars. Harbaugh and Anderson, however, were ineffective, and seemed on their way out.

The 1994 Bears hoped to show continued improvement. Once again, they contended for the divisional title—this time, all the way to the final week. The Bears had a chance to win the division, but a disappointing loss to the New England Patriots made them settle for a wild-card berth. After losing twice to Minnesota during the regular season, the Bears beat the Vikings on the road at the Metrodome in Minneapolis. Unfortunately, the San Francisco 49ers ended the Bears' season that year in the second round of the playoffs.

§

The Bears have always prided themselves as being the "Monsters of the Midway." Throughout their long and storied history, they have won championships with fearsome defenses and punishing ground games. Wannstedt is slowly restoring the bite in his defensive corps. Once the ground game returns, look for the Bears to emerge again atop the NFL.

**Chicago Bears coach Dave Wannstedt
watches his team at Soldier Field.**

GLOSSARY

ALL-PRO—A player who is voted to the Pro Bowl.

BACKFIELD—Players whose position is behind the line of scrimmage.

CORNERBACK—Either of two defensive halfbacks stationed a short distance behind the linebackers and relatively near the sidelines.

DEFENSIVE END—A defensive player who plays on the end of the line and often next to the defensive tackle.

DEFENSIVE TACKLE—A defensive player who plays on the line and between the guard and end.

ELIGIBLE—A Player who is qualified to be voted into the Hall of Fame.

END ZONE—The area on either end of a football field where players score touchdowns.

EXTRA POINT—The additional one-point score added after a player makes a touchdown. Teams earn extra points if the placekicker boots the ball through the uprights of the goalpost, or if an offensive player crosses the goal line with the football before being tackled.

FIELD GOAL—A three-point score awarded when a placekicker boots the ball through the uprights of the goalpost.

FULLBACK—An offensive player who often lines up farthest behind the front line.

FUMBLE—When a player loses control of the football.

GUARD—An offensive or defensive lineman who plays between the tackles and center or nose guard.

GROUND GAME—The running game.

HALFBACK—An offensive player whose position is behind the line of scrimmage.

HALFTIME—The time period between the second and third quarters of a football game.

INTERCEPTION—When a defensive player catches a pass from an offensive player.

KICK RETURNER—An offensive player who returns kickoffs.

LINEBACKER—A defensive player whose position is behind the line of scrimmage.

LINEMAN—An offensive or defensive player who plays on the line of scrimmage.

PASS—To throw the ball.

PASS RECEIVER—An offensive player who runs pass routes and catches passes.

PLACEKICKER—An offensive player who kicks extra points and field goals. The placekicker also kicks the ball from a tee to the opponent after his team has scored.

PLAYOFFS—The postseason games played amongst the division winners and wild card teams which determines the Super Bowl champion.

PRO BOWL—The postseason All-Star game which showcases the NFL's best players.

PUNT—To kick the ball to the opponent.

QUARTER—One of four 15-minute time periods that makes up a football game.

QUARTERBACK—The backfield player who usually calls the signals for the plays.

REGULAR SEASON—The games played after the preseason and before the playoffs.

ROOKIE—A first-year player.

RUNNING BACK—A backfield player who usually runs with the ball.

RUSH—To run with the football.

SACK—To tackle the quarterback behind the line of scrimmage.

SAFETY—A defensive back who plays behind the linemen and linebackers. Also, two points awarded for tackling an offensive player in his own end zone when he's carrying the ball.

SPECIAL TEAMS—Squads of football players that perform special tasks (for example, kickoff team and punt-return team).

SPONSOR—A person or company that finances a football team.

SUPER BOWL—The NFL Championship game played between the AFC champion and the NFC champion.

T FORMATION—An offensive formation in which the fullback lines up behind the center and quarterback with one halfback stationed on each side of the fullback.

TACKLE—An offensive or defensive lineman who plays between the ends and the guards.

TAILBACK—The offensive back farthest from the line of scrimmage.

TIGHT END—An offensive lineman who is stationed next to the tackles, and who usually blocks or catches passes.

TOUCHDOWN—When one team crosses the goal line of the other team's end zone. A touchdown is worth six points.

TURNOVER—To turn the ball over to an opponent either by a fumble, an interception, or on downs.

UNDERDOG—The team that is picked to lose the game.

WIDE RECEIVER—An offensive player who is stationed relatively close to the sidelines and who usually catches passes.

WILD CARD—A team that makes the playoffs without winning its division.

ZONE PASS DEFENSE—A pass defense method where defensive backs defend a certain area of the playing field rather than individual pass receivers.

INDEX